973.9
CRA

973.9
CRA

20TH CENTURY USA

History of the 1910s

Rennay Craats

WEIGL PUBLISHERS INC.

Published by Weigl Publishers Inc.
123 South Broad Street, Box 227
Mankato, MN, USA 56002
Web site: http://www.weigl.com
Copyright © 2002 WEIGL PUBLISHERS INC.

Library of Congress Cataloging-in-Publication Data available upon request from the publisher. Fax (507) 388-2746 for the attention of the Publishing Records Department.

ISBN 1-930954-47-6

Printed and bound in the United States of America
1 2 3 4 5 6 7 8 9 0   05 04 03 02 01

Senior Editor
Jared Keen

Series Editor
Carlotta Lemieux

Copy Editor
Jay Winans

Layout and Design
Warren Clark
Carla Pelky

Photo Research
Joe Nelson

Photograph Credits

American Stock/Archive Photos: pages 6BR, 17, 24, 31, 43; Archive Photos: pages 3B, 16, 19, 20, 25, 27, 29, 33, 35; Bettmann/CORBIS: pages 8, 9, 34, 38, 39; Camerique/Archive Photos: page 15; CORBIS: page 22; Deutsche Presse/Archive Photos: pages 7BL, 18; DeWitt Historical Society/Cody Collection/Archive Photos: pages 3TR, 37; Frank Driggs/Archive Photos: page 41; George Eastman House/Nickolas Muray/Archive Photos: page 13; MPI/Hulton Getty/Archive Photos: page 32; Museum of the City of New York/Berenice Abbott/Archive Photos: page 14; National Archives of Canada: pages 7BR(C242), 23(C30944), 42(C242); Photofest: pages 3TL, 10, 11, 12, 40; Popperfoto/Archive Photos: pages 6BL, 26; Sasha Collection/Hulton Getty/Arhcive Photos: page 36; Topical Press Agency/Hulton Getty/Archive Photos: pages 21, 30; Underwood & Underwood/CORBIS: page 28.

Every reasonable effort has been made to trace ownership and to obtain permission to reprint copyright material. The publishers would be pleased to have any errors or omissions brought to their attention so that they may be corrected in subsequent printings.

![USA 1910s logo]

Contents

Entertainment 10

Fashion 36

Literature 24

Tariff Relief

Clothing Fire

Black Sox Scandal

SPIES

Atomic News

Studios at War

Melting Pot

Halley's Comet

Child Labor

Treaty of Versailles

The 1910s were a time of contradiction—the economy was booming, but there was labor unrest. It was a time for Americans to enjoy the "good life," but there was war. These contradictions make the teen decade even more intriguing. During the 1910s, there were countless fascinating people and events. Some of these events affected small numbers of people while others drew international attention. The unsinkable *Titanic* sank en route to New York, and the declaration of war turned the world upside down. The U.S. remained neutral at first, but it later took up arms to fight for the Allies. This war was like no other. New weapons devastated troops until they found ways to defend against them. On the homefront, businesses continued to operate to support the war effort. Women filled in for men who had gone off to fight. By the end of the war, many states had given women the right to vote.

20th Century USA: History of the 1910s dives into American life. It follows political stories,

Bryan Resigns

Movie Madness

Albert Einstein

Rail Tragedy

Irish Uprising

GISH SISTERS

South Pole Reached

War Over

such as Prohibition and the election of a new president, Woodrow Wilson. It also tells tales of sports scandals. The Black Sox disgrace rocked baseball, and the questionable amateur status of the country's most-loved Olympian caused controversy for decades to come. When they were not following their favorite teams, many

Americans danced the fox trot, drove around in their Model Ts, and watched the top stars on the silver screen. Charlie Chaplin, Fatty Arbuckle, and the Gish sisters kept U.S. theaters packed.

This book only briefly discusses a few of the many happenings of the teen decade. If you read about something that interests you, visit your library to

find out more. The Internet, encyclopedias, and other resource books are great places to start your investigation of the 1910s. Now turn the page and enjoy your journey through time.

1910

All eyes are on the sky. Some people are afraid while others are excited to see the comet. Turn to page 26 to find out more about Halley's return and the nation's reaction to it.

1910

A committee is formed to guarantee the rights of African Americans. Turn to page 32 to learn more about the NAACP.

1911

Norwegian explorers reach the South Pole. Read about their incredible journey on page 16.

1911

The days of relying on hand cranks are over. Electric starters make driving a snap. Find out more about this development on page 26.

1911

Theodore Dreiser is redeemed. The great success of his new novel brings his controversial first book back to the public. Learn more on page 25 about why his first book was banned.

1912

Jim Thorpe competes for Olympic gold and wins two medals. This amazing athlete is one of the best of the century. Why, then, did he lose his medals? Find out on page 29.

1912

The "unsinkable" ship is far from it. During its maiden voyage, the *Titanic* sinks. Page 8 has details about this disaster.

1913

The U.S. welcomes a new president. Woodrow Wilson is sworn into office after defeating William Taft. Find out more about the campaign and Wilson's leadership on page 20.

1913

Cars are rolling off the line in record time, thanks to Henry Ford's new system. Read about his assembly line on page 35.

1913

The Big Train powers through the competition. The Washington Senators' pitcher sets a record for the most shutout innings in the league. Turn to page 31 to find out more about this legendary athlete.

1914

The U.S. falls for the Tramp. The baggy-panted comic hero fills theaters and sets off a brilliant career. Find out more about Charlie Chaplin on page 12.

1914

The arrest of U.S. sailors nearly results in a war with Mexico. Page 42 details the rocky relationship between the U.S. and its neighbor to the south.

1914

Coal miners in Colorado have had enough. They walk off the job. Management is not sympathetic. Uncover the violent end to the strike on page 34.

Halley's Comet

The Big Train

1914

A single gunshot sparks a world war. Countries scramble to take sides in the brewing conflict. Page 18 has the story.

1914

Americans are fox-trotting the night away. Learn more about this dance sensation on page 14.

1916

Ireland declares independence, and Britain is not amused. Page 17 has the details of this uprising.

1916

The government aims to protect children with the Owen-Keating Law. This law would prevent children from being exploited in the workplace. Turn to page 23 to read about why the law failed.

1916

Battles rage across Europe as the Allies try to stop the **Central Powers**. Read about two significant battles on page 19.

1917

Uncle Sam declares war on the Central Powers. Despite trying to stay neutral, President Wilson assembles U.S. troops to join the conflict. Find out why on page 20.

1917

Russian citizens say "niet." Hunger and poor wages cause an uprising. To learn more about the revolution and its leader, Vladimir Lenin, turn to page 16.

1918

Booth Tarkington's "magnificent" book makes him a star. It also earns him a Pulitzer Prize. Page 24 has more about this writer's success.

1919

It is a dismal time for baseball. Eight Chicago White Sox players are banned from the league for life. Find out about the World Series scandal on page 30.

1919

Prohibition is passed, making manufacturing, selling, or consuming alcohol illegal. The country was dry. Page 21 has more about this law.

1919

Boston is deep in molasses. A strange and sticky disaster causes incredible damage and kills twenty-one people. Read more on page 9.

1919

The Treaty of Versailles is drawn up to punish Germany for starting the war and to compensate the countries affected. To find out who was involved and what the treaty stated, turn to page 42.

The Great War

The Treaty of Versailles

The Unsinkable Ship

*T*itanic was not only the world's largest ship—it was also the most luxurious. The $7.5-million ship was considered unsinkable—it had a double-bottomed hull divided into sixteen watertight compartments.

On April 10, 1912, 2,224 people boarded the ship for its first voyage from Southampton, England, to New York. Just before midnight on April 14, *Titanic* hit an iceberg south of Newfoundland, Canada. Few people noticed the bump, but the impact tore a huge hole in the side of the ship, and water flooded the lower levels. The captain ordered women and children into lifeboats. He also sent out distress calls. Since the ship's designers thought the liner was unsinkable, there were only enough lifeboats for half the passengers. People panicked. Some scrambled into available lifeboats, which were lowered half-full. Others frantically raced around the ship looking

■ A painting by Willy Stoewer, a German artist, depicts the sinking of the Titanic.

"After we had rowed away some distance, we saw lighted deck after lighted deck disappear, til there was nothing but the bleak level of the water with the starry sky lighting the spot where she sank from sight."

A survivor aboard one of the lifeboats

for more boats. The ship's band played until the very end.

Less than four hours after the collision, the "unsinkable" ship sank. About 700 people, mostly women and children, escaped in lifeboats and were later picked up by the *Carpathia*. But more than 1,500 people died in the frigid Atlantic Ocean. It was the worst maritime accident ever.

Mount Katmai Erupts

In January 1912, Alaska was the site of the biggest and most extensive volcanic eruption in North American history. Lava spewed from the volcano, located on the southern tip of the Alaskan Peninsula, and the cone collapsed. More than 7 cubic miles of cinder and ash were released during the explosion, covering an area as large as Connecticut. The effects of the dust and ash in the air were felt as far as Kodiak, 100 miles away. The Pacific Northwest was pelted with ash-laden rain for days. The eruption gave rise to a wasteland full of geysers, salt flats, mineral springs, and gas holes. It is now the Katmai National Monument.

Sticky Situation

On January 15, 1919, the unthinkable happened in Boston, Massachusetts. The north end of the city was home to a 90-foot-high tank that was 282 feet around. It was full of **molasses**, stored there by the Purity Distilling Company. On that day in June, people heard rumblings and explosions from the vat. Then it burst open, releasing a black river of molasses onto the streets—about 2 million gallons of molasses poured from the tank. The initial wave was 20 to 30 feet high and flowed faster than a person could run. The molasses knocked down buildings and drowned twenty-one people. Pieces of the tank flowed with the river, slicing through walls. Rescuers did not know how to help. They were knee-deep in thick syrup. Horses became trapped in the mess and had to be shot. Survivors had to have their sugar-crusted clothing cut from their bodies. Slowly, the city began a clean-up. The smell of molasses stayed in Boston for weeks, and the harbor was tinted brown for nearly five months. Investigations into the strange disaster found that Purity Distilling was guilty of poor workmanship on the tank. It was ordered to pay more than $1 million in damages.

■ An elevated train structure is a twisted mass of metal on Atlantic Avenue after the Great Molasses Flood of 1919.

RAIL TRAGEDY

■ July 9, 1918, marked the worst rail accident in U.S. history. Two trains collided head-on in Nashville, Tennessee. At 7:15 AM, a local train ran a stop signal and switched to the same track that an outbound express train occupied. The crash destroyed both locomotives, three baggage cars, and six passenger carriers. The wreck claimed 101 lives and injured 171.

Clothing Fire

The Triangle Shirtwaist Factory was one of thousands of **sweatshops** in New York. On the eighth, ninth, and tenth floors of the Asch Building, about 850 young immigrant women worked at sewing machines. The rooms were filled with cloth, tissue paper, and scraps of oil-soaked rags. The shop owners locked heavy steel doors to keep the girls at work.

On Saturday, March 25, 1911, a spark from a cigarette or sewing machine set some fabric scraps on fire. As the flames spread, the girls tried to escape, but the only door that opened was blocked. Several girls climbed out the window onto a fire escape that led to the roof, but it could not handle the weight. It twisted from the wall and fell to the street. Other girls panicked and jumped to their deaths. Firefighters' hoses could not reach the eighth floor, and their ladders were not long enough to save the workers. There were 145 dead—all but thirteen of whom were girls in their early teens. The tragedy caused people to push for new labor laws and better fire codes. Even so, a court later found the owners not guilty of manslaughter.

Entertainment

THE GISH SISTERS

Lillian and Dorothy Gish had been wandering from theater to theater playing child roles. Then the 16- and 14-year-old girls turned to Biograph Studios to make them famous. There, they became two of the first movie queens. In 1912, young women throughout the country tried to be like the Gish sisters, from the way they dressed to how they interacted with men. The real-life Gishes were far less glamorous. They signed on for long hours and earned $5 per day.

At times, shooting films was dangerous. In *Way Down East* (1920), Lillian floated down a river on an ice pack wearing only a thin dress. Her arm trailed in the icy water. The director shot more than 100 takes of that scene. Lillian credited being in shape and taking cold baths for her survival in these movies.

Both Lillian and Dorothy were praised for their acting. Dorothy found success in light comedies and pantomime, but Lillian became more of a star as she grew up. She starred in D. W. Griffith's movies, such as *The Birth of a Nation* (1915) and *Intolerance* (1916). She showed that she could adapt to different roles when she starred as a poor girl from the slums in *Broken Blossoms* (1919). After making several silent movies, Dorothy and Lillian each made one sound movie in 1930 and then returned to performing on stage.

Perilous Films

In 1914, a new kind of movie hit the theaters. Serials became popular with the help of Pearl White. Her character, Pauline Marvin, was a rich girl who needed adventure, and she always found it. White starred in twenty biweekly installments of *The Perils of Pauline*. In the exciting episodes, she defended against outlaw attacks, fell from cliffs, floated in a runaway balloon, and was aboard a ship that blew up. She was saved by her stepbrother and suitor, Harry, just in time, much to the relief of the enormous U.S. audience. Those who could not make it to the movie house could read about Pauline's adventures in local newspapers. The stories were printed at the same time as they were shown in the theaters. The success of *Pauline* led to many imitations.

The silent film serial *The Perils of Pauline* captivated audiences with its action and suspense.

Hollywood Tolerates Intolerance

In 1915, director D. W. Griffith's extravagance caught the attention of Hollywood. He built a huge set of towers and parapets, some standing as high as 90 feet. Griffith also gathered some of the top movie stars and about 15,000 extras for this project. Other directors and actors were very curious about what the director was up to. In 1916, everyone found out. The three-hour film called *Intolerance* left critics awestruck. Griffith's unusual camera angles and flashbacks made his films especially amazing. *Intolerance* is set in an exotic location and a timeframe ranging from modern-day America to ancient Babylon. The film cost nearly $2 million to produce. It was thought to be the greatest movie ever made, but audiences were confused by it. The plot was complicated and hard to follow—there were four separate story lines woven together. Although an amazing piece of filmmaking, *Intolerance* was a box office flop. It did not even come close to making its

"*Intolerance* is so colossal, gorgeous, and stunning to the mind that words fail."

A review in the *New York Tribune*

■ The city of Babylon in the movie *Intolerance* was the largest set ever built.

money back. Griffith's company, which had been created to make the movie, filed for bankruptcy in 1921. Despite its failure, other directors tried to match the movie's extravagance and technical achievements.

Chautauqua Draws Crowds

About 40 million people flocked to the tent shows, called Chautauquas, each summer during the 1910s. These shows were named after festivals held on Lake Chautauqua in New York and were put together by sponsors and agents. The presentations offered something for everyone—exciting bands, magicians, opera singers, yodelers, and lecturers. One of the biggest draws was inspirational speaker Dr. Russell H. Conwell. He told Americans how to make money by going no farther than their own backyards. Chautauquas traveled across the country during the summer. Signs, banners, and posters plastered towns for weeks before the tent went up. For many people who paid their twenty-five cents to go to the shows, this was their only exposure to live theater and music. It was the highlight of the year and a social event that could not be missed.

The Tramp

Charlie Chaplin was the king of silent movies. The Briton toured the U.S. in 1910 and decided to stay. In his 1914 film *Kid Auto Races at Venice*, he developed his much-loved character, the Tramp. His style was unique—it combined acrobatics, pantomime, elegance, and gestures. The Tramp was a symbol of the underdog coming out on top. When playing him, Chaplin wore baggy pants, huge shoes, and a bowler hat. He carried a bamboo cane as he walked. This character appeared in more than seventy movies. Chaplin brought the Tramp to a few different studios. He signed with the Mutual Company for $520,000 per year. When he re-signed with the company, he received $150,000 as a bonus. Chaplin's yearly earnings were seven times higher than that of the U.S. president. In 1918, Chaplin used his own studio to transform the Tramp from a slapstick character to one with compassion and depth.

Chaplin was more than a brilliant actor. He also was a talented producer and director, with such movies as *City Lights* (1931), *The Great Dictator* (1940), and *Limelight* (1952). He often starred in the movies he produced. In 1972, Chaplin was given a special Academy Award for his contribution to the industry, and he was knighted three years later.

United Artists Formed

In 1919, three of Hollywood's biggest stars joined forces to create their own movie studio. The three were "America's Sweetheart" Mary Pickford, Charlie Chaplin, and screen idol Douglas Fairbanks. They joined with legendary director D. W. Griffith to form United Artists. It was the first time that a studio was run by the actors and creative team behind the movies. The team would have complete artistic and financial control over their films. The stars all had contracts with other studios, which they had to fulfill before concentrating on United Artists. The studio lost money in the twenties, and Griffith left the studio, but hit movies from Chaplin and Fairbanks brought in enough money to keep the studio running. Good management helped as well. United Artists was a powerful force in Hollywood until the remaining founders—Mary Pickford and Charlie Chaplin—sold the company in the 1950s.

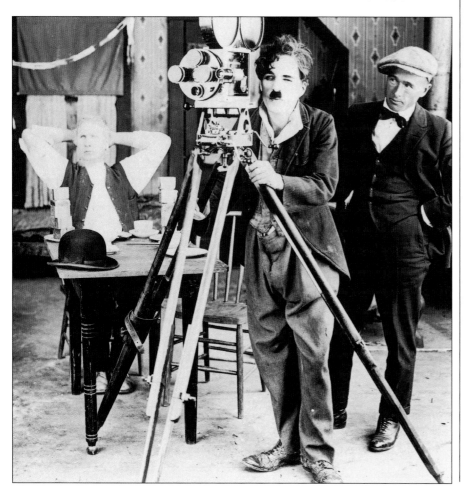

■ Charlie Chaplin was as talented behind a camera as he was in front of one.

Ziegfeld Follies

Florenz Ziegfeld, Jr., had been entertaining audiences with Broadway musicals since 1907. Elaborate sets, singing, and comedic acts made up the Ziegfeld Follies. The Follies helped create three famous stars—Fanny Brice, Irving Berlin, and Bert Williams. Brice was a far cry from the traditional Broadway star. This young girl was not beautiful and sweet, like most of the other Broadway girls. She had big eyes and a wide grin—most of all, she was funny. She sang comic songs with an exaggerated Yiddish accent. For her first performance in the Follies, Brice sang a song written by Irving Berlin. The song, "Goodbye, Becky Cohen," was one of many numbers prepared by Berlin over the years. In 1919, he wrote "A Pretty Girl Is Like a Melody,"

which became one of the best-known Follies songs. Another of the show's stars, funnyman Bert Williams, an African American, raised eyebrows, but Ziegfeld did not care. He put the best people on the stage, and Williams was the best. The glitzy **vaudeville**

■ The Ziegfeld Follies were known for their talented showgirls and outrageous costumes.

show ran for twenty-four years and has never been topped.

Studios at War

In 1889, Thomas Edison invented movies. He also held patents for the equipment and film processes. In 1909, he set up a trust that created a **monopoly** over U.S. film production. Other companies had the choice to join the trust or stop making movies. Many studios joined Edison's Motion Picture Patents Company. A few tried to fight it. Independent producers, including William Fox and Carl Laemmle, looked to the

New York courts to help them fight the trust. The trust fought back by refusing to ship films to movie houses that showed its rivals' movies. It also took movie cameras off the market to prevent these movie makers from being able to work. Independent studios were broken into, and film and equipment was destroyed or stolen. Movie shoots turned into brawls. Some independents left New York for California to escape the trust.

Even on the other side of the country, studios made movies secretly. Their safety and survival

depended on it. Equipment was still often stolen or destroyed. Directors and actors were beaten or even shot at. Some studios tried to put their rivals out of business by attracting their box-office stars. The formerly anonymous stars were offered enormous salaries to change studios. Despite the initial dangers, California soon blossomed as a filmmaking center, and countless directors, actors, and studios moved there to make their fortunes.

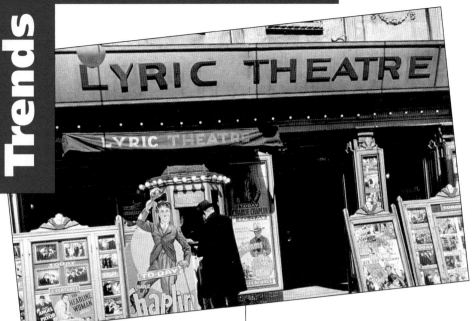

A man purchases a ticket for the Lyric Theatre, one of New York's earliest motion picture houses. It is still in use today.

the common, one-reel movie cost studios about $500 to produce in only a few days. By the end of the decade, producers were releasing two-hour feature films that cost up to $20,000 to make. The motion-picture business was no longer a struggling industry run by a few competing studios. It was the fifth largest industry in the country.

Movie Madness

In the 1910s, a night out at the theater no longer meant the opera or a play. Motion pictures were all the rage. Beautiful movie theaters were built. Patrons paid their quarter at the door and were welcomed with large, comfortable seats, elaborate decorations, and uniformed ushers. There was even a twenty-five piece orchestra to entertain them before the film began. Americans packed movie houses to watch the popular comedies and melodramas. For the first time, actors were recognized by name rather than by their studio. The "Biograph Girl" and "Vitagraph Girl" were finally revealed and became major box-office draws. Their huge salaries were met with huge profits. In 1916, about 25 million people each day paid between a dime and a quarter each to watch a movie. This brought more than $735 million to studios.

Producers used this money to create more sophisticated, high-budget silent movies. In 1910,

CARE TO DANCE?

Americans celebrated the good economic times in the early 1910s by crowding onto the dance floor. In 1914, the fox trot took over every dance hall in the country. It combined the energy of ragtime music with the elegance of high society. The fox trot became a symbol of modern Americans. The dance got its name from a vaudeville entertainer named Harry Fox, who added a trotting step to his routine. When the dance hit ballrooms, it involved two walking steps, a side step, and a quarter turn.

The fox trot had many variations. Well-known dancer Irene Castle and her husband, Vernon, created a faster and more subtle version of the dance. Legend has it that Castle's dress was too tight at the bottom to perform the dance as it was usually done, so the pair accidentally changed it. They used the "Castle walk" in Broadway musicals, cabarets, and dance demonstrations.

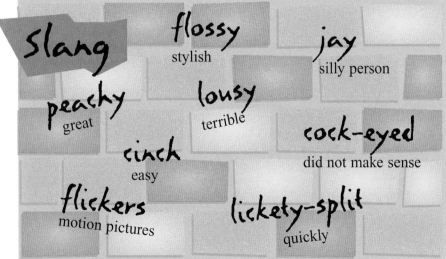

Slang

flossy
stylish

jay
silly person

peachy
great

lousy
terrible

cock-eyed
did not make sense

cinch
easy

flickers
motion pictures

lickety-split
quickly

In the Driver's Seat

Horses and buggies were quickly becoming a thing of the past. Automobiles were the way of the future. They were no longer just luxury items reserved for wealthy people. The Model T, produced by automobile maker Henry Ford, was a fairly low-cost car. In 1914, Ford produced 240,700 Model Ts—nearly as many cars as all the other automobile manufacturers combined. These cars, nicknamed Tin Lizzies, were simple machines, with strong steel frames. They were great on muddy streets and could travel at around 40 miles per hour on flat roads. If there were any problems with the car or its parts, drivers could easily fix them using the most basic tools—a screwdriver, hammer, wrench, and wire. Ford Motor Company even provided replacement parts. It sold mufflers for a quarter and a whole bumper for $2.50. As Ford streamlined his factories, the price of a Model T dropped. By 1916, Americans could drive one home for only $360. By the end of the 1910s, 4 million Tin Lizzies were puttering around U.S. streets.

A man demonstrating one of the first changeable wheels on a Model T Ford.

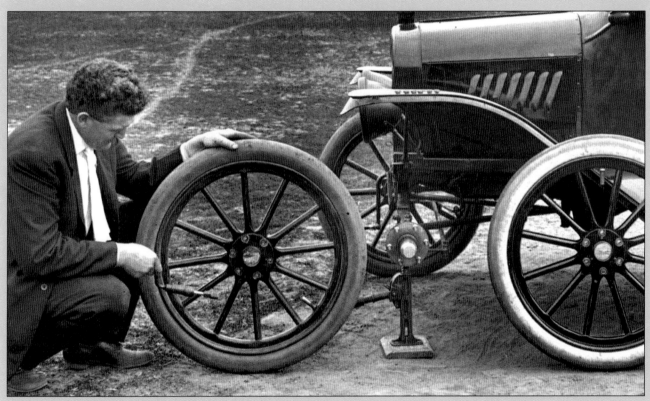

Fun and Games

Before the 1910s, most stores carried toys only at Christmas time. By the end of the decade, toys and games were on store shelves year-round. Transportation toys were popular. The friction auto racer was a toy car that could climb. It ran backward and forward. Toy airplanes were on many boys' wish lists as well. The airplanes flew in circles as their propellers whirled. A milk wagon with turning rubber wheels was another hit with children. Building kits, porcelain dolls, board games, and magic sets also delighted U.S. children. One of the most popular toys of the 1910s was the Humpty Dumpty Circus. The small figures of lion tamers, clowns, trick riders, elephants, and other circus animals could all be arranged in different ways with their movable heads and limbs.

First to the South Pole

As a child, Norwegian Roald Amundsen was fascinated by the Arctic. In 1906, he became the first European to sail through the Northwest Passage, and he wanted to be the first to get to the North Pole, too. Robert Peary beat him to it in 1909, so Amundsen did the next best thing—he went to the South Pole. In 1910, Amundsen set off on a ship with nineteen people, ninety-seven sled dogs, four pigs, and six pigeons. Then the five-person exploration team traveled 1,860 miles from the Bay of Whales to the South Pole without any trouble. They completed the journey exactly on schedule. The team had everything it needed—so much so that the explorers gained weight during the four-month trek. They traveled across dangerous glaciers and mountains, all the while battling temperatures as low as –76° Fahrenheit. Amundsen's team finally reached the South Pole on December 14, 1911. They planted a Norwegian flag at the bottom of the Earth.

Russian Revolution

■ Russian communist leader Vladimir Ilyich Lenin stands before a crowd of revolutionaries in St. Petersburg, Russia, in April 1917.

World War I was destroying Russia. The **tsar's** government had fallen. The economy was in shambles, and people were starving. In February 1917, 200,000 Russians took to the streets. The crowd would not disperse, even when attacked by police. As more workers joined the revolution, the demonstrators became bolder and more aggressive. Some soldiers obeyed the order to fire at the demonstrators, but most refused and joined the people. The revolutionaries had won, and the monarchy was overthrown. A temporary government was established in Russia. Although it had the people's support, no one could agree on what type of political system the new state should use. Then the Bolshevik Party, led by Vladimir Lenin, took charge. On October 25, the Bolsheviks took over the Winter Palace and the government. The following day, Lenin set up a Soviet government. This new government confiscated private land and gave it to the state. It also took control of banks, the transport system, and industries. In March 1918, the Soviets pulled Russia out of World War I by signing a peace agreement with Germany. There was civil war in Russia, though, and anti-Bolshevik groups gained popularity. Over the next two years, millions of Russians were killed, and much property was destroyed. In the end, Lenin's group won but at the cost of many lives.

Continental Drift

In 1912, German scientist Alfred Wegener explained something that had puzzled scientists for years. He explained why the coastlines of the world's Eastern and Western hemispheres look as though they would fit together. He proposed that all seven continents had, at one time, been one large landmass. He called this supercontinent Pangaea. Pangaea eventually split apart, he said, creating the modern continents. To support this theory, known as "continental drift," Wegener collected fossils and rocks that were found only in South Africa and Brazil—areas that would have originally been one region. He also matched mountain ranges by piecing the continents together again.

Many people doubted Wegener's theory, for he could not explain why the continents began to shift. Despite the criticism, Wegener continued to work on his theory. He died in 1930 without sufficiently explaining continental drift. In the 1960s, scientists developed theories to support Wegener's ideas. His studies gave rise to **plate tectonics**, which shifted the focus of geological study.

> "In the name of God and of the dead generations from which she receives her old tradition of nationhood, Ireland, through us, summons her children to her flag and strikes for her freedom."
>
> Patrick Pearse on the steps of the post office

▬ Fighting spilled into the streets during the Easter Rebellion as Irish patriots battled British police.

Irish Uprising

It was a quiet Easter in 1916 until a group of Irish nationalists took over the Dublin post office and declared Ireland independent from Britain. The group was led by rebel Patrick Pearse, who stood on the front steps of the post office and announced that they had taken over the city. The rebels were part of two patriotic groups, the Irish Republican Brotherhood and the Irish Volunteers. This Easter Uprising was short-lived. Within a few days, the British army set up in key positions in Dublin and began shelling the area around the post office. Pearse surrendered, and he and other rebels were arrested. More than 450 people were killed, and 2,614 were wounded in the conflict. Few people had supported the rebellion at first.

Then, once it was over, British Commander in Chief Sir John Maxwell ordered that fifteen rebels be executed. He arrested and jailed members of Sinn Fein, the nationalist organization that he assumed had **orchestrated** the rebellion. This led to renewed patriotism in Ireland. People rushed to join Sinn Fein, making it a powerful political organization in the country. The rebels were regarded as heroes who had died trying to free Ireland, and the centuries-long struggle between Britain and Ireland continued.

Assassination Sparks War

■ Archduke Franz Ferdinand, with his wife, Sophie, just minutes before their assassination in Sarajevo, Serbia.

The first shots of World War I were fired when Gavrilo Princip squeezed the trigger of his gun aimed at Archduke Franz Ferdinand and his wife. On June 28, 1914, the heir to the Austro-Hungarian throne was visiting Sarajevo. As he rode through town in an open car, a bomb was thrown at him. Ferdinand knocked it aside and it exploded away from the car. Later in the day, Princip fired three shots into the car, killing the archduke and his wife, Sophie. Austro-Hungarian investigators linked the assassin to a Serbian terrorist group. They insisted that Serbia stop all threats to Austro-Hungarian rule. They also ordered that anti-Austrians be arrested. Serbia refused these demands and asked that an outside body intervene to help calm the situation. Austria-Hungary refused.

On July 28, Austria-Hungary declared war on Serbia. Serbia had the backing of Russia, France, and Britain. Germany supported Austria-Hungary. On July 29, Russia ordered its troops to be ready for action, and within two days, Germany declared war on Russia. On August 3, Germany declared war on France, which had begun to **mobilize** troops as well. Germany invaded Luxembourg and announced that it was going to march through Belgium, which was neutral, and attack France. This caused Britain to declare war on Germany on August 4. Within a month, many other countries became involved in the war. Within two months, 17 million soldiers were enlisted. The largest war in history spread across three continents—Europe, Africa, and Asia.

LIFE IN THE TRENCHES

■ By Christmas 1914, many people realized that the war was not going to be over quickly. They also realized that it was not as honorable a fight as they had thought it would be. Millions of soldiers were killed, injured, or missing on both sides. Germany moved forward with its plan to take France first. To do so, it had to get through Belgium. With Britain's assistance, Belgium fought to block Germany's advance. It failed. German forces reached the Marne River near Paris, but the French were not going to give up. They pushed the Germans back and then dug in, literally. Both countries saw that fighting on open ground was not working. Each army dug lines of trenches from which soldiers could launch attacks. They lived in appalling conditions, sharing the muddy trenches with rats and lice. The trenches stretched for hundreds of miles from the English Channel to Switzerland. Bombs had destroyed nearly everything around the trenches, leaving soldiers in a barren wasteland.

Bloody Battles

In 1916, two terrible battles in France caused hundreds of deaths and showed the senselessness of war. The Battle of Verdun, which began in February, occurred as Germany fought the Allies for control of Verdun, France. Germany wanted to keep the French troops occupied so that Britain would be left on its own. By April, France had control of the air and was better able to defend the area. Then the Allies launched an **offensive** on the Somme River. The First Battle of the Somme drew German forces away from other posts. This allowed Allied troops at Verdun to advance and reclaim land lost to Germany. The allies pushed the Germans back and moved the lines to where they had been in February. The Somme offensive lasted from July to November. The Allies eased pressure at Verdun and gained a small amount of land at the Somme. The bloody battle ended when winter rains turned the battlefield into swampland. These battles were costly. The Verdun battle claimed 600,000 Allied **casualties** and 450,000 German casualties. The Somme conflict took almost 350,000 French lives and killed 330,000 Germans. These battles were seen as a turning point for the Allies in the war.

Allied troops in a trench prepare their bayonets for battle.

The War Is Over!

Germany wanted to win the war before U.S. forces in Europe were up to full strength. In 1918, German troops broke through lines of trenches that had been set for four years, resulting in an incredible loss of life on both sides. With 10,000 U.S. troops arriving per day, the Allies counterattacked. The Germans retreated. At the same time, the Bulgarians were forced from Serbia and the Austrians were ousted from Italy. Meanwhile, the Central Powers were arguing with one another about how to divide the conquered lands once the war was won. There were also strong peace movements in their home countries. The Allies were exhausted and were experiencing supply shortages, so they decided to follow one commander, Marshall Ferdinand Foch. This unity led to victory. Bulgaria surrendered on September 30. The Ottomans surrendered on October 30, and Austria-Hungary agreed to peace on November 3. Germany was alone. On November 11, 1918, World War I ended when the Germans signed a peace agreement. This victory came after four years and three months of terrible battles and bloodshed. More than 37 million people died during World War I.

Wilson Elected President

In 1912, Woodrow Wilson became the country's leader, but he did not have majority support. He had won the presidency with only 41.9 percent of the popular vote. Even so, the majority of Americans shared his attitudes and opinions. He promised African Americans that they would be treated fairly under his leadership. He also promised workers that he was on their side and was sympathetic to their concerns. He would improve working conditions, he said, and decrease the power of monopolies. Wilson's campaign promises, along with his friendly, down-to-earth personality, made voters trust him. He took 435 of the electoral votes, while his opponents won only 96. Wilson's government had a majority in both houses of Congress. Once elected, he began to make social reforms. He also turned the U.S. away from **isolation** and toward more involvement in foreign affairs. This led to America's participation in World War I. Wilson was re-elected president in a narrow victory in 1916.

■ President Wilson speaks to a summertime crowd.

Uncle Sam Joins the War

"The world must be made safe for democracy."

President Wilson

On May 7, 1915, the British passenger liner *Lusitania* was carrying people and war supplies from New York to Great Britain. It was torpedoed off the coast of Ireland and sank. The German U-boat, or submarine, attack killed approximately 1,200 of the 1,900 passengers and crew, including 128 U.S. citizens. Americans were outraged, and anti-German feelings swept the country. Many people wanted the U.S. to declare war on Germany, but President Wilson wanted to keep America out of the war. This proved difficult when, in 1917, Germany stated that it would destroy any ship that was near any Allied country. By the middle of March 1917, three U.S. ships had been torpedoed by German U-boats.

Then the U.S. intercepted a telegram from Germany to Mexico offering assistance in taking back Arizona, Texas, and New Mexico. The message was likely a set-up, but Wilson reacted nonetheless. On April 6, 1917, he declared war on Germany. U.S. involvement in the war strengthened the Allies and helped defeat the Central Powers.

Dry Country

Many groups in the U.S. had been trying to get alcohol banned since the 1800s. In 1919, Congress finally passed the eighteenth amendment. This made manufacturing, selling, or transporting "intoxicating liquors" illegal. Many people completely supported the new law. They thought that drunkenness was to blame for violence, family breakdowns, and poverty. By the time this law, called Prohibition, was officially enacted, thirty-three states, accounting for 63 percent of the population, had already passed their own state laws against alcohol. But this did not stop everyone from drinking. **Bootleggers** secretly sold alcohol, and illegal clubs provided a place to drink. Despite this, consumption of alcohol did go down considerably. Although Prohibition ended in 1933, consumption did not return to pre-Prohibition levels until 1975.

■ Men destroy wine and spirits in Boston during Prohibition.

I SPY

■ Support for the Allies turned into anger against Germany. This feeling exploded when German spies were discovered in the U.S. On July 24, 1915, a secret service agent obtained a briefcase from German agent Dr. Heinrich Albert. The contents of the case showed that Albert had been given $28 million by the German government to disrupt U.S. society. German spies had started fires, staged "accidents" at munitions plants, set off bombs on ships, and tried to start strikes in key industries such as steel production. Soon, U.S. citizens were imagining they saw spies at every corner. Many foreign-born people were arrested or sent back to their country of origin. Only a small number of the people targeted and punished were found to have been spies.

Bryan Resigns

William Jennings Bryan helped Woodrow Wilson get elected in 1912. As a reward, he was made secretary of state. Bryan negotiated thirty treaties with other countries and earned himself a solid reputation as a diplomat. But above all, Bryan was a strong pacifist—he did not want to see the U.S. drawn into war. After the sinking of the *Lusitania*, he feared the worst. He saw President Wilson going back on his vow not to get involved. The government was adopting the anti-German feelings that were strong throughout the country, and Wilson was taking steps to prepare to enter the Great War.

Bryan resigned his post to show his disapproval of the government's change of heart. Once the U.S. entered World War I, Bryan supported the war effort, but he did not rejoin the government. Instead, he practiced law and was a special prosecutor in the Scopes Trial, supporting **creationism** against evolution in the 1920s.

Propaganda Machine

During World War I, the government established a special agency called the Committee on Public Information. Its aim was to convince Americans that the U.S government was doing the right thing so that people would support it in the war against Germany. About 75,000 men, called "four-minute men," delivered short patriotic speeches at theaters across the country. Meanwhile, congress passed wartime laws against spying and speaking against the government. There were serious penalties for saying negative things about the Constitution, the flag, the government, the military, or any Allied country. Citizens could receive a $10,000 fine or twenty years in prison for purposely slowing down the production of war goods.

The laws affected education and freedom of the press as well.

"Victory is a Question of Stamina," a World War I Poster by Harvey Dunn.

Victory is a Question of Stamina
Send – the Wheat
Meat · Fats · Sugar
the fuel for Fighters

History professors and historians taught the Allied version of history—that Germany was totally at fault for World War I. Magazines and newspapers also had to support the government's actions. About 6,000 people were arrested for disobeying these laws. About 1,500 were sentenced after being found guilty of such offenses as criticizing the Red Cross or the YMCA. Such a suspension of Americans' rights would have been unimaginable before the war. The panic about spies and pro-German plots prompted many people to approve of these measures.

FOURTEEN POINTS AND THE LEAGUE OF NATIONS

After World War I, President Wilson wanted a peace that would last. He presented fourteen points, or peace proposals, to Congress on January 8, 1918. These points included abandoning secret agreements between countries, removing international trade barriers, and deciding what to do with conquered territory. Some of the Allies disagreed with a number of Wilson's points—some points went against their colonial and territorial interests. His final point was to develop an organization of nations to ensure peace. This later became the League of Nations. Wilson insisted that the entire package be accepted. After presenting the proposals at the peace conference in Paris, Wilson returned home. When he flew back to Paris to sign the treaty, he found that the Allies were discussing returning Europe to its prewar state. Wilson fought to reintroduce the league into discussions. At home, the Senate was torn over the treaty. Some wanted to add more conditions. Others were completely against the treaty because they felt it was a matter for Europeans to decide. Wilson did not want conditions. He hit the streets to defend the covenant across the country. Wilson's health was poor and he suffered a stroke. On November 19, 1919, the Senate rejected the treaty altogether. The U.S. never became a part of the League of Nations.

Campaigning for the Vote

For decades, a small group of U.S. women had been appealing to successive governments for the right to vote. In the 1910s, that group became larger and stronger. Women gathered at marches and rallies and made speeches about their rights. They lobbied Congress, met at tea parties, and attracted more supporters. Actresses, including Lillian Russell, joined the cause. **Suffrage** was fashionable. Many people, mostly men, were against giving women the vote. They thought that women would not understand the importance of voting and should stick to "feminine" concerns, such as housework and fashion.

Hundreds of thousands of women rallied for the vote. Slowly, state governments agreed to give women the right to vote in state elections. By 1920, women had the right to vote and to run for federal political office. With the nineteenth amendment, about 26 million voters were added to the ballot list.

Stopping Child Labor

In the U.S. in the 1910s, about 13 percent of the workers in the textile industry were under the age of sixteen. This was of concern to many people in society and government. In 1916, Congress passed the Owen-Keating Law. This legislation made it illegal to buy or sell goods made in factories that employed children under fourteen years of age. The law also applied to factories where children between the ages of 14 and 16 worked more than eight hours per day. However, the law was ruled unconstitutional in 1918—the Supreme Court said that it violated personal freedom. The next year, Congress tried again to protect children in the workplace by taxing employers. This Child Labor Tax was soon ruled unconstitutional as well. By 1924, both houses of Congress passed a constitutional amendment that opened the door for Congress to regulate, limit, and prevent children under 18 years of age from working. Only twenty-eight states agreed to the law—eight fewer than the number required for a change in law. The fight to keep children in school rather than at work continued for decades. By the thirties and forties, the laws were finally considered constitutional and child labor was restricted.

Child mine-workers worked hard for very little pay.

Western Writer

Zane Grey once worked as a dentist in Zanesville, Ohio. He soon turned from teeth to books. In 1904, he wrote his first book called *Betty Zane*. It was based on his ancestors' experiences. From there, he carried on this family story with *The Spirit of the Border* in 1905. Grey then began writing stories about the frontier and Wild West. With the release of *Riders of the Purple Sage* in 1912, Grey became a literary legend. This book sold 2 million copies and was made into a movie three times. Even though he wrote more than eighty novels, *Riders of the Purple Sage* was his best-known work. The novel followed ideas that appeared in many of Grey's stories— the struggling outlaw who fought for good and found love in the process. Readers got an accurate sense of history from Grey's books. Although some people criticized his romanticized plots, they could not deny the historical description and research that went into his novels. Grey's novels sold 17 million copies in his lifetime and more than 100 million copies worldwide throughout the century. Zane Grey's novels, and the movies, comic books, magazines, and radio and television programs they inspired, entertained Americans throughout the 1910s and beyond.

King of the Bookstores

For fourteen years, Edgar Rice Burroughs had tried unsuccessfully to make his name in business. Then he decided to try his hand at literature. He found he was much better at writing than at business. His 1914 novel, *Tarzan of the Apes,* was an exciting and exotic adventure story that Americans loved. The title character was the son of a wealthy British family. He was orphaned in the African jungle and was raised by a group of apes. The novel followed the adventures of Tarzan and Jane, the daughter of a scientist. There were more than twenty Tarzan books, which were translated into fifty-six languages. More than 25 million copies of the Tarzan books have been sold around the world. Tarzan was more than a character in a

■ Along with his *Tarzan* series, Edgar Rice Burroughs wrote several science fiction and crime novels.

book—he became a folk hero. The adventures of Tarzan, king of the jungle, appeared on radio and television, at the movies, and in comic books.

MAGNIFICENT LITERATURE

■ Booth Tarkington was one of the most popular and widely read novelists of the era. His books included many humorous works for young people. *Penrod* (1914) and *Seventeen* (1916) were two such hit comedic novels about young boys. Between 1902 and 1932, Tarkington's work made its way to the bestseller list nine times. Among his best work was his adult novel *The Magnificent Ambersons* (1918). This novel won him the first of his two Pulitzer Prizes for fiction—the other was for *Alice Adams* (1921). Like many of his novels, *The Magnificent Ambersons* was set in his home state of Indiana. It was the story of three generations of the wealthy and influential Amberson family. Tarkington explored their greed, self-centered attitudes, sophistication, and ultimate failure. Both of the author's prize-winning novels were made into movies in the thirties and forties. Tarkington wrote more than forty novels during his career.

Robert Frost

In 1912, poet Robert Frost sold his farm, quit his teaching job at the New Hampshire State Normal School, and moved his family to Britain. He met influential poets there who helped him publish his work. His first two poetry volumes, *A Boy's Will* (1913) and *North of Boston* (1914), received rave reviews. This new style of poetry spoke from the heart. Frost wrote of his experiences in New England and about U.S. values. News of his European success and his reputation as a talented poet had already arrived when he returned to the U.S. in 1915. Frost continued to publish poetry and went back to teaching literature at many prestigious schools, including Harvard University. He won the Pulitzer Prize four times, beginning in 1924. He was also

 Robert Frost's best-known poem is "The Road not Taken."

the first person to read a poem at a presidential inauguration— he read "The Gift Outright" for President John F. Kennedy in 1961.

American Novelist

In 1900, reporter and editor Theodore Dreiser turned his attention to fiction with the novel *Sister Carrie*. It was the story of a girl who moves to Chicago and then becomes a Broadway star in New York. People were outraged by the novel. Some of its characters were terrible, immoral people who showed no remorse for their actions. The publisher removed the book from store shelves. This did not stop Dreiser from writing. His magazine work earned him a solid reputation. By the time his second novel appeared in

1911, he had some very influential supporters. *Jennie Gerhardt* was different from his first work. This was the story of a moral, upstanding woman who was hurt and disappointed by a harsh and cruel society. She had a child without being married, was thrown out by her father, and was cast aside by her wealthy lover. The novel was a huge success, prompting *Sister Carrie* to be reissued. Dreiser became well-known for his 1925 novel, *An American Tragedy*, which told the story of a real-life murder case.

BESTSELLERS

When deciding what to read, many Americans consulted the bestseller list. Since 1895, this list had offered reviews and named the most successful books. The list was based on book sales, so some classics never made it to the list. For example, Sherwood Anderson's Winesburg, Ohio *(1919) did not sell well but was considered an American classic. Below are the bestsellers of the 1910s.*

1911 **The Broad Highway**
by Jeffrey Farnol

1912 **The Harvester**
by Gene Stratton Porter

1913 **The Inside of the Cup**
by Winston Churchill

1914 **The Eyes of the World**
by Harold Bell Wright

1915 **The Turmoil**
by Booth Tarkington

1916 **Seventeen**
by Booth Tarkington

1917 **Mr. Britling Sees It Through**
by H. G. Wells

1918 **The U.P. Trail**
by Zane Grey

1919 **The Four Horsemen of the Apocalypse**
by V. Blasco-Ibanez

1920 **The Man of the Forest**
by Zane Grey

START YOUR ENGINES

■ Before 1911, automobile drivers had to use hand cranks to start their vehicles. Charles Franklin Kettering's electric starter put an end to that unpleasant, unreliable, and potentially dangerous practice. Many people thought that such a device was impossible. They figured that a motor capable of turning over a car engine would weigh too much and would not allow the car to carry passengers. Kettering recognized this problem as well, but he also realized that the starting motor did not have to run the automobile. He created a small generator and motor unit. The motor was run by a storage battery. It had just enough power to start the engine. Once the engine was running, it powered the generator, which powered the battery. Kettering had proven the world wrong. His system was a success, and Cadillac became the first company to use self-starting cars.

■ Halley's Comet has captivated stargazers for centuries.

Halley's Streaks across the Sky

On May 18, 1910, more people were on their rooftops than inside their homes. Many people were afraid of what they saw. Others were fascinated. The object of these mixed emotions was Halley's Comet. Astronomers and scientists had been eagerly awaiting the arrival of the comet for decades. It appeared approximately every seventy-six years. A German astronomer finally located the comet in 1909, and people waited for it to become visible to the naked eye. Many citizens were not as eager. They did not understand the comet and believed that gases from the comet's tail could cause serious damage to Earth's atmosphere and could even harm people. Tabloid newspapers fed the fear around the world with terrifying and inaccurate stories about the comet. Some people refused to

Diagnosis Affects Thousands

African Americans had been suffering from a blood condition that no one could identify. The condition led to serious infections, injury to major organs, and extreme pain throughout the body. In 1910, a Chicago physician figured out the problem. Dr. James Bryan Herrick examined a West Indian student who had these symptoms. He found that the student had unusually shaped red blood cells. These cells looked like a crescent-shaped farm tool called a sickle. The cells could not pass through tiny blood vessels, so oxygen and other nutrients were withheld from organs and other parts of the body. This is what caused the pain and organ damage. Herrick called the disorder sickle-cell anemia. This disease was in about 3 percent of the African-American population.

go to work around the expected time of the comet's arrival— they wanted to stay with their families. In reality, the trail of gases stayed about 250,000 miles from the surface of our planet. Astronomers collected any information they could from the passing comet, knowing that they would have to wait many years to study it again.

New Weapons of War

World War I was made even more horrible by the new weapons developed to fight it. The Germans relied on their stealthy U-boats to sink enemy ships. The U-boats were not invincible, though. The newly developed depth charge could be fired at a submarine, German U-boats were forced to strike quickly in order to avoid a depth-charge attack.

The first widespread use of aircraft occurred during World War I. The Germans used **zeppelins** to bomb Britain. In the fifty-five attacks, more than 700 people, mostly civilians, were killed—these airships could not fire accurately. While they often aimed at military targets, the bombs did not always fall there. The British army also used airships to bomb the enemy. Pilots released bombs over enemy territory by pulling a string. Small planes guided the heavily armed bombers. Fighter pilots earned recognition and fame as they fought in the air. Some pilots, such as Germany's Manfred von Richthofen, also known as the "Red Baron," became legendary.

Of all the new weapons, poisonous gas was the most inhumane. Germany used the gas for the first time on Russian troops in January 1915. The Allies followed their lead and developed their own dangerous gases. Both sides wore masks during gas attacks to protect against inhaling the fumes. New gases that penetrated the skin were soon developed. These gases killed soldiers in trenches slowly and painfully.

Theory of Relativity

Albert Einstein became a household name when he announced his theory of relativity in 1916. The theory had been eleven years in the making. It built upon Isaac Newton's theory about space and time, and it created a new way of looking at the universe. He explained that if he was correct, a ray of light passing across the Sun's surface would bend twice as much as Newton had said it would. In 1919, a solar eclipse confirmed Einstein's prediction and his theory. He remains one of the most influential physicists ever.

■ Einstein's theories continue to influence our understanding of physics and nature.

WORLD FOCUS

ATOMIC NEWS

British physicist Ernest Rutherford was no stranger to the scientific world. He had won the Nobel Prize for Chemistry for his study of radium. In 1911, he changed the way the world perceived atoms. Before then, scientists thought atoms were solid. Rutherford sent positively charged helium particles toward a sheet of gold foil. Most of these helium particles went through the foil with ease. This proved that most of the space taken up by an atom was empty. Some particles were blocked by the foil, which showed that some of the atoms had mass. Later, Rutherford discovered that oxygen was produced when helium particles were sent through a nitrogen atom. This led to the discovery of nuclear energy.

Athletics Rule the Diamond

The Philadelphia Athletics won the World Series championships in 1910, 1911, and 1913. They also battled for the title in 1914 and 1915. Frank "Home Run" Baker was one reason for the success. He was one of the year's top five home run hitters in the American League seven times. He was also at the top for runs batted in. But Baker was not only an offensive player. He was a great infielder as well. For seven years, he put out more players than any other third baseman. During his rookie year in 1909, he earned a .305 batting average and led the league in triples. Baker's two home runs and .375 series average led the Athletics to the championship in 1911. In 1913, he hit twelve home runs, 117 runs batted in, and had an average of .450 during the World Series match up. Baker played for the Athletics

■ The Philadelphia National Team in Ebbet's Park, Brooklyn, at the opening of the 1913 season.

until 1916. He was traded to New York and finished his career as a Yankee.

Pitcher Charles "Chief" Bender was another key Athletic during the 1910s. Rather than work his way through the minor leagues, he shot directly to the top of the majors. On May 12, 1910, he delivered a no-hitter to the Cleveland Indians, thanks to a new pitch he had developed. It was a hard curveball that became

known as a slider. His strong arm helped the team win the championship. He was the first pitcher to have six championship titles under his belt. Bender retired in 1917, finishing his career with an impressive earned run average of 2.46 and with 212 wins and 127 losses to his name.

Forward Pass

Before the success of its football team, the small South Bend, Indiana, college of Notre Dame was virtually unknown across the country. Then star players Knute Rockne and Gus Dorais arrived and put the school on the sports map. Notre Dame's

team was small, and the coaches were looking for a way to make up for that. Rockne, the team captain, suggested they try the forward pass. The forward pass had been used since 1906, but it was not often brought into college play. As a result, few other teams would know how to defend against this strategy. In a game against fearsome Army,

Notre Dame's forward passing proved itself a huge success. Notre Dame beat the larger and stronger team 35 to 13. This upset launched the school to the top of the football ranks and changed football forever. More teams began using the forward pass, making it a basic part of the game.

Racing for Victory

Ray Harroun liked speed. He earned his living at it. In 1911, he entered the history books at the first Indianapolis 500. At the time, the automobile race was called the International 500 Mile Sweepstakes. On May 30, 1911, Harroun started his engine in twenty-eighth position on the track. Six hours, forty-two minutes, and eight seconds later, Harroun crossed the finish line, having traveled at an average speed of 74.602 miles per hour. He was the first winner of the prestigious race. He took home $10,000 of the total $25,000 prize money for the race. Since 1911, the Indianapolis 500 has been run every year except during World War I in 1917 and 1918 and again during World War II from 1942 to 1945. Today, the race draws more than 350,000 spectators, who watch 33 drivers circle 500 miles around the track.

Short-Lived Hero

Jim Thorpe was one of the greatest athletes in the 1910s. This Native American from Prague, Oklahoma, could do it all—football, baseball, lacrosse, archery, hockey, boxing, and tennis. In track and field, Thorpe was unbeatable. He could run, throw, and jump better than anyone else in the world. That was proved at the 1912 Olympic Games. Thorpe came out on top after an exhausting three-day decathlon competition. He set a world record score of 8,412.955 points. He won another gold medal in the pentathlon event. When he returned from the Olympics, Thorpe was greeted as a star, but his status as the first great Olympic hero soon faltered.

Six months after the Olympics, it was discovered that Thorpe had earned $25 a week playing minor-league baseball during the summers of 1909 and 1910. This made him a professional athlete and not eligible to compete at the Olympics. Thorpe's appeal to the Amateur Athletics Union was refused. His gold medals were taken from him, and his records were erased. The athletes who had finished second supported Thorpe. They refused to accept the gold medals. Despite the controversy, Thorpe was voted the best athlete of the first half of the century in 1950. He went on to play professional baseball in Boston and New York and football in Canton, Ohio. In 1982, long after his death, the International Olympic Committee restored Thorpe's records and then presented the gold medals to his children the following year.

■ Jim Thorpe was inducted into the National Football Foundation's Hall of Fame in 1951.

OLYMPIC MEDALS

■ Several U.S. athletes brought medals home from the 1912 Summer Olympic Games in Stockholm, Sweden. In shooting events, Alfred Lane won three gold medals and Frederick Hird won two gold and one bronze medal. In the pool, Americans showed their strength as well. Duke Kahanamoku took first in the 100-meter freestyle contest, while Harry Hebner swam for gold in the 100-meter backstroke. In track, Ralph Craig earned two gold medals in the 100- and 200-meter races. In the 100-meter, there were seven false starts. In one of these, Craig had already sprinted to the finish line before being called back. Despite this, he raced to victory. Other U.S. champions rode bicycles. The cycling team took the bronze medal, and Carl Schutte won the bronze in the 200-mile cycling event.

Golf for the Public

Before 1913, golf was a game reserved for wealthy people. That changed when Boston's Francis Ouimet stepped onto the green. The twenty-year-old unknown golf caddy entered the U.S. Open tournament. Both amateur and professional golfers could compete in this tournament. He defeated prominent British golfers Harry Vardon and Ted Ray in eighteen holes to win the tournament. This is thought to be one of the largest sport upsets of the twentieth century. Besides earning Ouimet a reputation as a

talented golfer, the victory brought international attention to both the tournament and the sport. Members of the general public became interested in golf and began playing and watching it. Golf's popularity soared. In 1916, the Professional Golfers' Association of America (PGA) was established, and annual tournaments began immediately. More golf courses were built to accommodate the soaring interest in the sport.

Francis Ouimet prepares for a golf match by practicing on a rooftop in London, England.

Black Sox Scandal

There was no disputing it—the Chicago White Sox was one of the greatest baseball teams ever to walk onto the field. The talented athletes played for little money, often about $4,000 per season. They worked "regular" jobs in the off-season to support themselves and their families. In 1919, many of the White Sox players became frustrated because they were making piles of money for the team's owner and for gamblers—but not for themselves. The players wanted a piece of the pie.

Chick Gandil, Sox first baseman, spoke to gamblers about putting money up for a fix. He asked for $100,000 for the players to intentionally lose the World Series. Everyone would bet on the Sox to win, and the gamblers could bet on the Cincinnati Reds and make an easy fortune. The gamblers agreed. Gandil got to work.

He needed enough men to agree to throw the games in order for the scam to work. He thought that eight would be enough. He approached eight key

> **"Say it ain't so, Joe."**
> A disbelieving fan

players, and seven agreed to take part. As the Series was played, rumors about a fix floated around. Some sports writers began watching the games closely, marking errors that seemed unusual.

The scandal was finally revealed. Seven White Sox players, including pitcher Eddie Cicotte and fielder Shoeless Joe Jackson, were banned from professional baseball. An eighth player, Buck Weaver, was banned because he had known about the scam but had not come forward. The team became known as the Black Sox, and the incident marred baseball.

The Big Train

Walter Johnson was one of the best major league pitchers in history. He was nicknamed "The Big Train" because he could throw the ball so fast. He signed with his team, the Washington Senators, in 1907. The team was not a top club, but Johnson managed to build an impressive record anyway. He won 417 and lost 279 in his career. This achievement was topped by only the legendary pitcher Cy Young, who finished his career with 511 wins. During Johnson's career, he prevented the other team from scoring a single run 110 times, which was a league record. In 1913, Johnson set a Major League record with fifty-six shutout innings. This feat also earned him the American League's most valuable player title and thirty-six wins for the season.

The main reason for Johnson's shutout games was his fastball. Batters could not hit what they could not catch up to. He led the American League in strikeouts an amazing twelve times, including in 1910 and from 1912 to 1919. His career strikeouts number 3,509. This record held until 1983, when Nolan Ryan passed this number. Johnson retired from playing in 1927 and managed professional teams from 1929 until 1935. In 1936, Johnson was honored with an induction into the Baseball Hall of Fame.

■ Walter Johnson pitched for twenty-one seasons before retiring.

SIR BARTON UNBEATABLE

■ In horse racing, all horse owners and jockeys wanted to win the Triple Crown. This meant winning the Kentucky Derby, the Preakness Stakes, and the Belmont Stakes all in the same year. This had not happened since 1875. In 1919, jockey Johnny Loftus riding Sir Barton, a chestnut colt, swept these prestigious races to achieve the unthinkable—the Triple Crown title. Sir Barton, named after the first Australian prime minister, was an amazing horse and was the first great thoroughbred racer in the U.S. No other horse could remove Sir Barton from the top. It took until 1930 for another horse to claim victory in all three events and to become a Triple Crown winner. There have been only eleven horses in history that have won this honor.

WORLD FOCUS

DROPPING THE PUCK

In 1917, the National Hockey League was established. It consisted of only Canadian teams. The league was home to four teams—the Montreal Canadiens, the Montreal Wanderers, the Toronto Arenas, and the Ottawa Senators. That year, the Wanderers' arena burned to the ground so they had to withdraw from competition. That left only three teams to battle to the championship. Toronto beat out the Montreal Canadiens to win the first title of the "Champions of the World." In 1924, the Boston Bruins, longtime supporters of amateur hockey, became the first U.S. team to join the NHL. By 1926, six of the ten teams were from the U.S., including teams from Detroit, Chicago, and New York.

■ Since its creation, the NAACP has become a powerful civil rights organization.

Fighting for Equality

For a decade, riots against African Americans had plagued the U.S. In 1910, sixty scholars gathered to form a committee to do something about it. This committee became the National Association for the Advancement of Colored People (NAACP). The organization's co-founder, Mary White Ovington, promised to try to bring the country together in an atmosphere of tolerance and justice. Although the Civil War had freed people from slavery, it had not given them rights. African Americans were segregated from Americans of European descent and could not go to the same restaurants, schools, or many other places. The NAACP fought racism and prejudice through education and in the courts.

Before 1915, "grandfather clauses" had prevented African Americans from voting because many of their grandfathers had been slaves and were unable to vote. Then, the U.S Supreme Court voided the laws that said that in order to vote, a man's grandfather must have voted. For the rest of the century, the NAACP brought about important changes. This new movement inspired African Americans across the country to come together and stand up for their rights. It also led to human-rights awareness around the world. By 1954, the NAACP had caused the segregation laws to be declared unconstitutional. At that time, it was the largest civil rights organization in the world with 500,000 members.

SAY CHEESE

■ By the 1910s, cameras had become reliable as well as easy to use. By 1913, shutterbugs could buy an inexpensive camera for $2—down from $25 for a Kodak camera. For $6, photographers could use a pocket-sized Autographic Kodak produced by George Eastman. This camera allowed photographers to open a slot and add a caption to the photo they had just taken. This feature cost Eastman $300,000 to patent. The new photography craze led to many professional photographers carrying their cameras around to record life in the U.S. Photo studios opened in every city and town, where people could have formal portraits taken. They could also have photographs of special occasions, such as baby arrivals, birthdays, anniversaries, and weddings. As well, it was now easy to take candid or casual photographs. For the first time, people could record their everyday lives in snapshots.

Lending a Hand

Millionaire John D. Rockefeller tried for three years to establish a charitable foundation. Rather than giving to only one cause, he wanted to form an organization that would fund experts in many fields who were trying to make the world a better place. Rockefeller wanted his foundation to join forces with the federal government, but Congress was suspicious. The government had judged his Standard Oil Company an illegal monopoly, and the politicians thought his charitable foundation was a way of restoring his reputation and gaining influence over the government. Rockefeller dropped his federal charter and aligned the foundation with New York State instead. In 1913, the Rockefeller Foundation was finally up and running. Rockefeller's foundation supported medical research. He financed malaria-control programs and helped create better medical schools in sixty-two countries. Other foundations, including the Carnegie Corporation, also tried to give back something to society. Andrew Carnegie focused his dollars on education and social research. He funded studies of race relations that led to important changes. Many other U.S. millionaires and billionaires have continued the tradition of great philanthropists such as Carnegie and Rockefeller.

■ John D. Rockefeller gave more than $540 million to charitable groups.

The New Woman

The 1910s brought with it a new kind of woman. She abandoned restrictive clothing and social rules. She was independent and demanded equality with men. These women drove automobiles, cropped their hair short, wore makeup, and threw conservative ideas to the wind. Men at the time were not sure how to take this new, strong woman. When the U.S. entered the war, these were the first women to take over men's jobs in ammunition factories and other industries. Some even joined the navy as **stenographers** and clerks.

Some men, including magazine editor H. L. Mencken, supported their efforts. He said these women were beautiful and charming as well as strong. Other men were terrified by the change. They thought that women should remain at home to take care of children. Many women also questioned why others would try to be so "masculine." Working, smoking, and drinking were all traditionally men's areas, but women took them by storm. At the beginning of the decade, about 7.5 million women worked outside the home. By 1920, the number was 8.5 million and was steadily rising.

Striking Out

As many as one-half of U.S. laborers worked twelve-hour days often seven days a week. They were paid very little for their efforts. Many people lived in slums near the factories at which they spent most of their time. They wanted a six-day workweek and better working conditions. In the 1910s, workers began to take steps toward labor reform, and strikes and unrest swept the country. Large companies were threatened by the strikers' demands. The companies felt their property rights were at risk. As a result, strikers were met with violent company guards, brutal strikebreakers, and at times police forces that sympathized with the companies. In Colorado, 9,000 striking coal miners stayed off the job for more than a year and a half. In 1914, a group of company guards attacked the strikers' camp armed with guns. They killed at least twenty-one people and injured one hundred.

From January to June 1916, there were more than 2,000 strikes and lockouts. In 1917, striking members of the Industrial Workers of the World, a radical union, were taken from their beds at gunpoint, forced into trucks, and dumped in a

New Mexican desert with minimal food and water. They were later imprisoned until the strike was broken. Other members of this union were beaten or even lynched. The path toward reform was slow and difficult, but the strikers' actions

Labor rights activist Alexander Berkman speaks at an Industrial Workers of the World meeting in New York City.

helped lay the groundwork for future labor legislation in the U.S.

FAIR PRACTICE

The government stepped into business in 1914 by establishing the Federal Trade Commission (FTC). This independent body replaced the Bureau of Corporations. Members of the Commission were appointed by the president with Senate approval. To ensure fairness, no more than three of the five members could be from the same political party. The FTC set out to make sure that business practices were fair in order to protect the interests of everyday Americans. The commission targeted such offenses as price-fixing, misleading advertising, false labeling of products, unfair competition, and poor quality products. Its job was to make sure that Americans could make choices based on facts. If a business was guilty of engaging in any these practices, the commission could order it to stop doing so. If it refused, the business could be taken to court. The FTC also gathered information about the economy and business for Congress and the president.

Rolling Down the Line

Automobile makers, such as the Ford Motor Company, produced 160,000 cars per year. In 1913, Henry Ford tried something new at his Highland Park, Michigan, plant. He introduced the assembly line, which was based on the process lines of Singer sewing machine and Colt firearms plants. Ford's assembly line was a bit different. Unlike process lines, Ford's conveyor belt did not wait for a whole process to be completed. Instead, workers performed the same, small task on the line as the automobile part passed by. Employees had to work quickly and could not rest or the piece would pass before they had done the necessary task.

Ford's new system made skilled workers unnecessary. Before, a skilled worker had completed a single magneto wheel in twenty minutes. Now, twenty-nine unskilled workers finished the same job in thirteen minutes—each employee turned a screw or made an adjustment as the wheel rolled down the line. The time was later decreased to five minutes. The assembly line brought about the eight-hour shift and a five-dollar day. This was double the average wage before the assembly line. The company could afford such wages because it was making so many cars. Once Ford's assembly line was perfected, one Model T was rolling off the line every twenty-four seconds. This allowed for an incredible increase in production. It also brought car prices down. Model Ts dropped from $850 in 1908 to $440 in 1914.

■ Workers on a Ford assembly line piece together a Model T.

Tariff Relief

One of President Wilson's top priorities was to lower **tariff** rates. He wanted to break down monopolies that were protected by the high tax that other countries had to pay when importing goods into the U.S. He wanted to prevent U.S. companies from charging high prices because there was no competition. Wilson did not want to wait for these reforms, so he pushed the bill forward quickly. The Underwood Tariff was prepared and ready for the president's signature by October 1913. This bill cut taxes on imported, manufactured, and semi-manufactured goods. The average tariff dropped from 41 to 27 percent. In addition, the bill got rid of taxes on most raw materials. For instance, the import tax on sugar was eventually removed. This was the first time that tariffs had been reduced since before the Civil War. Wilson's bill also provided for a tax on income to replace some of the money lost due to lower tariffs. World War I slowed U.S. trade with other countries. The issue of tariffs did not become a hot topic again until the economic slump of 1920 and 1921. At that time, customs taxes were increased to levels higher than had ever been seen before.

DANDY GENTLEMEN

■ In the early 1910s, designers created new looks for U.S. men. The most fashionable men were seen around town in a one- or three-button coat or a double-breasted straight-hanging jacket. Pants became wider, measuring about 22 inches around the bottom of the pant legs. Men wanted to look "dandy." To dress up for the evening, a fashionable man carried a cane and wore a high-collared jacket set off with a bow tie. To finish off the look, a bowler or other style of hat was a must.

Younger men and boys also had new looks in the 1910s. They often wore three-piece suits for evenings out. The pants fitted the wearer snugly and had reinforced or double knees. High stockings met the bottom of the pants so no skin showed. These styles were all replaced with more casual and practical fashions once the war began.

Arden's Style

Florence Nightingale Graham was a secretary in New York City when she read Alfred Lord Tennyson's 1864 poem "Enoch Arden." She loved it so much that she changed her name to Elizabeth Arden in 1910. Under this new name, she opened a beauty salon with a bright red door as an invitation. The salon was on ritzy Fifth Avenue. Her salon was incredibly successful, so she opened more stores. The red door became a symbol of quality cosmetics that were very "ladylike." Arden insisted on that. She soon released a makeup line that came to boast more than 300 items. By the time of her death in 1966, Elizabeth Arden was a fashion legend with more than 100 salons carrying her name.

■ Elizabeth Arden's style influenced fashion around the world.

Tight-fitting Fashions

In the 1900s, women had worn tight undergarments called corsets that pinched and made breathing difficult. In the 1910s, they discarded these pieces of clothing. The bodices that replaced them were similar to corsets but looser and bloused out. This gave clothing a more natural look. It also allowed women to show their natural body shape rather than squeezing themselves into corsets. For the first time, women's comfort was considered when determining the latest fashions. This comfort revolution, however, did not last long.

In 1912, other fashion restrictions appeared on store racks. Skirts were designed to fit very tightly at the ankle. By 1914, skirt-bottoms were so tight that women could barely walk. Fashionable women were forced to take tiny, stuttered steps—that was all the material would allow. Designers began adding slits and pleats in the fabric. This gave the appearance of a narrow style while allowing women to walk with a more normal stride. Even with these improvements, the dresses were impractical. Stepping up to a streetcar or even climbing stairs became an incredible challenge. Many women hoped that wide-bottomed dresses would become fashionable so that they could move and walk more easily.

Straight Style

Before the 1910s, dresses often had extra material bustled down the back. Now dresses flowed smoothly and hung softly over women's bodies. Dresses were also almost completely straight. The most eye-catching feature of the new look was the length of the dresses. Day dresses were shorter, exposing the wearer's ankle. Some were even a few inches above the ankle. Some older women disapproved of this style. They thought it was dishonorable for a woman to show so much of her legs in public. Younger women loved the revolutionary fashions and bought straight dresses in droves.

Men also enjoyed the straighter styles. The days of over-starched, crisp suit shirts were over. Shoulder pads were removed from jackets to allow the jacket to fall straighter on the body. Suits and jackets became more fitted, and comfort became a consideration for men as well. Men even abandoned their lace-up boots for soft, comfortable oxford shoes.

Headwear

Women in the 1910s began cropping their hair in bobs. During the war, female factory workers found longer hair a nuisance. While many younger women chose shorter styles, others kept the curls made famous by the actress Mary Pickford. Women who wore their hair short used fancy combs, hairpins, barrettes, and other clips to accent an outfit or to pull their hair back with style. Traditional longer hairstyles were often worn piled on top of the head under a hat or gathered in a twist at the nape of the neck.

Headgear was an important item. The finishing touch to evening wear was a beautiful headpiece. Some women used strips of material studded with jewels to match their evening gowns. These hair bands resembled crowns or tiaras, and they were often trimmed with a feather. In 1912, dancer Irene Castle introduced U.S. women to embroidered caps. They became a fashion necessity. Most women had several hats, suitable for various occasions.

■ Irene Castle wears a sequined head ornament in the film *Patria*.

"There is here a great melting pot in which we must compound a precious metal. That metal is the metal of nationality."

President Wilson

The Melting Pot

President Woodrow Wilson said the U.S. was like a melting pot—newcomers arrived and then "melted" into American society. Most of the immigrants in the pot during the early 1910s were from southern and eastern Europe— about 1 million people arrived in the U.S. from these areas each year. One-quarter of the elementary schools in the country were filled with immigrant children, but these people were not integrating. In 1913 alone, 538 foreign-language newspapers were introduced. Halls and national alliances popped up across the country—the New York Czechs met in the huge National Hall, and the Polish National Alliance had hundreds of branches. Many newcomers to the U.S. realized the importance of their nationality after they left

their home countries. Not all Americans supported this tie to foreign roots, especially with the increasing hostilities in Europe. They demanded that these people "melt" and abide by slogans such as "America first." Immigrants were expected to support their new home first or return to their country of origin.

■ Customers in a U.S. shop purchase *marcouck*, a type of Syrian bread.

The rift between foreign-born and U.S.-born citizens increased as World War I progressed.

Asians Barred from Citizenship

Many immigrants faced discrimination and violence in the 1910s. Newcomers from India, although a small number, were chased from cities by mobs of angry Americans. Residents claimed that these Asians were not good citizens and would never fit into U.S. society.

In 1917, Congress passed a general immigration act that limited entrance into the U.S. The Asiatic Barred Zone resulted. This Far East region included most of eastern Asia and the Pacific Islands. Congress ruled that no immigration from that area would be allowed. This policy was not removed until the Immigration and Nationality Act of 1952.

Hyphenated Americans

Even before the U.S. officially joined the war, its citizens were suspicious of new Americans. The country had spy fever. People thought anyone not born in the U.S. might be a spy. Immigrants who had arrived from countries represented by the Central Powers were immediately targeted. German Americans, Hungarian Americans, Austrian Americans, and Jewish Americans were all singled out. They were labeled "hyphenated Americans," which meant that they were loyal to two areas. Because of World War I, German Americans were feared most. In 1917, there were more than 2 million Americans who were born in Germany. Millions more were born in America of German parents. Before the war, these people were valued as upstanding citizens. As the war spread, German Americans were regarded as being **treasonous**. Employers were asked to check the national background of their workers to confirm loyalty to the U.S. Many German Americans lost their jobs.

Theodore Roosevelt pushed to make hyphenated Americans "100 percent Americans." Immigrants and Americans of foreign background were expected to abandon their traditional beliefs, customs, and languages. To be accepted, newcomers to the country had to leave their ancestry behind.

COMING TO AMERICA

■ Although immigration to the U.S. fell from the previous decade, many people still arrived in America in the 1910s. Below are some of the countries these people came from and their estimated numbers during the 1910s:

Italy	1,109,524
Russia	921,201
Canada	742,185
Austria-Hungary	559,763
United Kingdom	341,408
Mexico	219,004
Greece	184,201
Ireland	146,181
Germany	143,945

Literacy Tests a Must

In 1917, Congress passed a law that made literacy tests part of the immigration process. This had been debated for twenty years and had been turned down by three presidents. Those people against such tests argued that educated people were more likely to rise up against the U.S. government. Others argued that educated people would have the ability to carry out acts of sabotage. Some people fought the law because it would reduce the pool of unskilled, inexpensive labor in the country. President Wilson's final veto was overridden in February 1917. Now, any potential immigrant over 16 years old needed to prove he or she could read and write before being allowed into the country.

■ German suspects are arrested in New York City during World War I.

Singing the Blues

African-American composer W. C. Handy took the blues from being a little-known Southern style of music to having international appeal. He achieved this with a song called "St. Louis Blues" in 1914. Handy's song was a combination of ragtime and this new style, blues. He drew on the beautiful melodies from African-American folklore. He put notes together in a way different from that of other composers—he often used tones that fell between the major and minor scales. His compositions invited musicians to improvise, which eventually led to jazz music. Handy was a very talented cornet player. Although he was blind, he conducted his own orchestra. Other popular Handy songs included "Memphis Blues" (1912), "Beale Street Blues" (1917), and "Loveless Love" (1921). Handy later established a music publishing house and wrote and edited many books.

Ragtime King

As a child, Irving Berlin sang on street corners for pennies. Then he began publishing and performing his own songs. At the age of 22, Berlin wrote a song that made him famous. "Alexander's Ragtime Band" spread Berlin's name throughout the world in 1911. Although the song was not true ragtime, he became known as the "Ragtime King."

■ Despite his lack of formal training, Irving Berlin went on to musical greatness.

Americans loved the new, modern-sounding song. In the first seven months of the song's release, it sold a million copies of sheet music. By the end of the year, Berlin was a very wealthy man. He insisted that what made him a success was that he wrote American songs. Other composers at the time were trying to copy European music and style. Berlin refused and introduced the country to a sound that they could relate to. This was only the start of the young New Yorker's career. He went on to write songs for Ziegfeld's Follies and then established his own music publishing company. In the seventy years he worked, he wrote more than 1,000 songs, including "There's No Business Like Show Business" and "White Christmas."

JELLY ROLL MORTON

■ Born Ferdinand La Menthe, Jelly Roll Morton was the first person to write down jazz arrangements on music paper. When he was only 17 years old, Morton wrote his first song, "New Orleans Blues." It became a favorite cover song for the city's bands. Musicians and the public were amazed by Morton's unusual combination of ragtime, Creole, and Spanish music. In 1912, one of his best-known songs, "The Jelly Roll Blues," was published. In 1915, Morton moved to California. There he performed with the Spikes Brothers and established his own bands. His compositions, including "King Porter Stomp" and "Mournful Serenade," became jazz classics and earned him a reputation as the originator of the style.

In the 1910s, a song's success and popularity was not determined by record sales. It was determined by the number of copies of sheet music it sold. The music publishing houses hired full-time composers and lyric writers to produce hit songs. The publishers then launched marketing campaigns to boost the sales of the sheet music, which often had attractive covers to lure buyers. New York was a major sheet-music center. West 28th Street between Broadway and Sixth Avenue was nicknamed "Tin Pan Alley." It was here that many music publishers had their offices. In time, "Tin Pan Alley" came to refer to all publishers of popular U.S. sheet music across the country. In 1910, Tin Pan Alley boasted $2 billion in sheet music sales. Ragtime beat out the ballad as the number-one most marketable type of song. In 1914, the blues stormed Tin Pan Alley thanks to W. C. Handy. During World War I, production on Tin Pan Alley slowed, and jazz musicians left the area to find work. In the process, they spread blues and jazz to other areas of the country. Tin Pan Alley was important in making hit songs until the 1950s. Bill Haley and His Comets' smash "Rock Around the Clock" was the first international hit. By then, the fact that a song had been created in Tin Pan Alley had become less significant. A song's greatness was now determined by the number of records sold.

All That Jazz

The first jazz recording was made in New York City by a New Orleans group called the Original Dixieland "Jass" Band. This group of musicians released the record *The Darktown Strutter's Ball* in 1917. The new style caught on quickly both in the U.S. and overseas. The Original Dixieland "Jass" Band was an unlikely choice for the first recording—most of the exceptional jazz musicians of the time were African Americans. Rumors suggested that some of the jazz greats of the time, including Jelly Roll Morton and Buddy Bolden, had turned down the opportunity to record an album. They were afraid that other musicians would steal their

The Original Dixieland "Jass" Band, (L-R): Harry Ragas, Larry Shields, Eddie Edwards, Dominic James "Nick" LaRocca, and Tony Sbarbaro, 1917.

improvisations if their music was immortalized on records. The Original Dixieland "Jass" Band, on the other hand, was eager to make the recording. Its leader, cornet player Nick LaRocca, insisted he was a key player in the development of jazz. Despite the fact that the band was not skilled at improvising, and its rhythms were forced, jazz became immensely popular throughout the country.

Treaty of Versailles

At the end of World War I, Germany and the Allies signed an agreement called the Treaty of Versailles. The details of the peace agreement were negotiated at the Paris Peace Conference beginning January 18, 1919. The U.S., Great Britain, France, and Italy all attended the conference. Even though the decision would affect Germany greatly, there was no representative from that country at the meetings. In the first part of the treaty was the Covenant of the League of Nations. This created the first global peacekeeping organization. The league would enforce the decisions and negotiations that arose from treaties after World War I. The Treaty of Versailles ordered Germany to give up 10 percent of its territory to France and Poland and to pay damages to France and Belgium. Among other conditions, Germany had to agree to reduce the size of its military. Germans were generally unhappy with the agreement. It remained a source of anger for twenty years, and this anger led to World War II. The treaty was ratified on June 28, 1919. The U.S., however, did not sign the agreement. Instead, it signed a separate Treaty of Peace with Germany on August 25, 1921, in Berlin.

■ Officials gather to ratify the Treaty of Versailles.

Trouble South of the Border

Since 1910, Mexico had experienced revolution after revolution. Americans with property or businesses there wanted the government to send troops in to protect their interests. Instead, President Wilson decided to protect U.S. interests by encouraging a constitutional government in Mexico.

Wilson would not recognize Mexico's leader, General Victoriano Huerta, because he had taken power illegally. The U.S. supported Venustiano Carranza, who gained political strength with this U.S. backing. Regardless, Huerta maintained control.

In April 1914, U.S. sailors were arrested at Tampico by Huerta's security force. The men were released, but Wilson was enraged. He demanded apologies from Huerta's government, even though he would not recognize it. When the U.S. discovered that a German ship full of ammunition was on its way to the Mexican leader, Wilson sent troops to Veracruz. In the clash that followed, more than 300 Mexicans and 90 Americans were killed or wounded. Immediately, public opinion in Mexico turned against the U.S.

Close to War

In 1914, Mexican leader Venustiano Carranza overthrew President Huerta, but that did not help U.S. interests in the country. The new leader would not abide by the findings of mediators who were investigating the Veracruz killings. Wilson then turned his eyes to opposition leader Francisco "Pancho" Villa. That did not work out either. Villa tried to get the U.S. to invade Mexico so that he could take power. To anger the U.S. government into action, he raided U.S. towns near the border. In October 1915, Wilson decided to recognize Carranza as leader of Mexico. Villa reacted by kidnapping and killing Americans in January 1916. Then he crossed the border into Columbus, New Mexico. There he murdered U.S. citizens and set the town on fire. Wilson responded by sending 6,000 troops to Mexico and had Carranza's permission to search for Villa. Villa escaped and crossed the border again. He killed more Americans in Glen Springs, Texas. This almost caused a war between the countries. To calm the situation, a constitutional government was established in October 1916. Wilson brought his troops home, but relations between the neighbors were strained.

■ Pancho Villa and his revolutionary fighters prepare to battle U.S. forces.

Mixed Messages

President Wilson concentrated on America's relationship with other countries. He began an agreement that offered Colombia a $20 million payment for the role America had played in Panama's revolt against Colombia. The agreement became final in 1921. This brought anger from former President Theodore Roosevelt, who had encouraged Panama to break away from Colombia and become independent. Roosevelt resented Wilson's virtual apology for his previous policy. Regardless, President Wilson's government wanted to show that it wished to maintain friendly relations within North and South America.

Some of Wilson's actions did not support this claim of goodwill. Wilson and his secretary of state, William Jennings Bryan, approved actions that threatened Nicaragua's independence. They wanted to build a new canal, and they feared that the part of Nicaragua best suited for a canal would be taken over by European powers. In 1913, the U.S. government drafted a treaty that restricted the actions of the Nicaraguan government and allowed for U.S. involvement in the area. This **imperialistic** move was criticized by many people because it carried on President Taft's policies in the area. A year earlier, Marines had arrived in Nicaragua to stop a revolt against the U.S.-backed president, Adolfo Diaz. They remained there until 1933.

American Events of the 1910s

How well do you know the 1910s? Try this quiz.

1. What flooded Boston in 1919?

2. Charlie Chaplin, Fatty Arbuckle, and Gloria Swanson were all part of which movie company?

3. Where was the Easter Uprising?

4. Why were the laws restricting child labor overturned several times?

5. How many points were in President Wilson's peace covenant?

6. What had people terrified to look to the sky on May 19, 1910?

7. How many copies of the Tarzan books were sold?

8. Who developed the Theory of Relativity?

9. Who was the first professional pitcher to win six World Series championships?

10. Who was the first to record a jazz album?

Answers: 1. molasses; 2. Keystone Film Company; 3. Dublin, Ireland; 4. they were ruled unconstitutional; 5. fourteen; 6. Halley's Comet; 7. 25 million; 8. Albert Einstein; 9. Charles Bender; 10. Original Dixieland Jazz Band.

Choose the right answer:

1 Irving Berlin was:
a) a U.S. scientist.
b) the "Ragtime King."
c) charged with treason.
d) a British author.

2 The Melting Pot:
a) used scrap metal to make weapons and war supplies.
b) was part of the Chautauqua show.
c) was the process of making immigrants Americans.
d) was cracked in 1917.

3 Charlie Chaplin's famous Tramp character:
a) used gestures and expression.
b) relied on verbal comedy for laughs.
c) appeared in three films.
d) was turned into a comic book.

4 The attack that killed Archduke Ferdinand:
a) was orchestrated by one of his own officers.
b) was launched by guerrilla troops
c) was the second assassination attempt of the day.
d) drew the U.S. into World War I.

Answers: 1. b); 2. c); 3. a); 4. c).

True or False

1. D. W. Griffith's landmark film *Intolerance* was an enormous box office success.

2. Strikers were often met with violence from managers.

3. One of the Chicago White Sox players was banned from the major leagues not for throwing the series but for knowing about the fix.

4. At the Triangle Shirtwaist Factory fire, all but thirteen girls were saved.

5. Making movies was a dangerous affair in the 1910s.

Answers: 1. False. It was a critical success but a flop with audiences. 2. True 3. True 4. False. One hundred and forty-five girls died, all but thirteen of them were barely teenagers. 5. True

Newsmakers

Match the person in the news with his or her claim to fame.

1. founder of cosmetics company

2. inventor of electric car starter

3. German spy

4. popular novelist

5. blues musician

6. secretary of state

7. first person to the South Pole

8. co-founder of the NAACP

9. home-run king

10. trendsetting dancer

a) Mary White Ovington
b) Frank Baker
c) Roald Amundsen
d) W. C. Handy
e) Irene Castle
f) Charles Franklin Kettering
g) Heinrich Albert
h) William Jennings Bryan
i) Booth Tarkington
j) Florence Nightingale Graham

Answers: 1 j); 2 f); 3 g); 4 i); 5 d); 6 h); 7 c); 8 a); 9 b); 10 e).

atoms: tiny basic building blocks of matter

bootleggers: people who sell alcohol illegally

casualties: members of the military who are killed or injured during combat

Central Powers: the military partnership between Germany, Turkey, and Austria-Hungary during World War I

imperialistic: countries that acquire and control other countries, often for financial gain

isolation: inward-looking, separate from others

mobilize: to organize people or resources to be ready for action

molasses: the thick, sticky, sweet syrup produced during the refining of raw sugar

monopoly: sole control or possession of something, often refers to an area of industry

offensive: an attack, assault, or siege

orchestrated: organized a situation or event unobtrusively so that the desired outcome was achieved

plate tectonics: the theory that the Earth's crust is made up of several separate slabs which move independently

stenographers: people whose job involves writing shorthand and typing up reports and letters from shorthand copy

suffrage: the right to vote in political elections

sweatshops: places where people work long hours for little pay in poor conditions

tariff: a charge for importing or exporting

treasonous: acting against one's country

tsar: an emperor of Russia, before 1917

vaudeville: light entertainment show consisting of a variety of acts

zeppelins: German airships

USA 1910s Learning More

Here are some book resources and Internet links if you want to learn more about the people, places, and events that made headlines during the 1910s.

Books

Brewster, Todd and Peter Jennings. *The Century for Young People*. New York: Random House, 1999.

Eaton, John P. and Charles A. Haas. *Titanic*. New York: W. W. Norton, 1999.

Estrin, Jack C. *American History Made Simple*. New York: The Stonesong Press, 1991

Evans, Harold, *The American Century*, New York: Alfred A. Knopf, 1998

Internet Links

http://users.tibus.com/the-great-war/

http://silent-movies.com

http://www.mediahistory.com/time/1910s.html

http://www.costumegallery.com/1910.htm

For information about other U.S. subjects, type your key words into a search engine such as Alta Vista or Yahoo!